minorca
cooking and gastronomy

Photography: Oriol Aleu
Cookery and styling: Ana Torrontegui
Texts: Xim Fuster and Manel Gómez
Graphic design and layout: Joseta Torrontegui

TRIANGLE ▼ POSTALS

Acknowledgements:
Narcís Bonet, De Vins, Favi, Aleix and Mª Dolors, Dani and
Reme, Pepe and Car, Maria Esperanza Fuguep, Hort de Sant
Patrici, Panaderia Orfila, Racó de Cas Sucrer, Nando, Lutz
and Sol, Toni Monne, Luca Pagliari, Oriol Roset and to every-
one at the stalls of the Maó market.

© 2005, Triangle Postals S.L., Pere Tudurí, 8
07710 Sant Lluís, Menorca

Edition and project coordination: Oriol Aleu
Graphic design and layout: Joseta Torrontegui
Cookery, styling, recipe adaptation and revision: Ana
Torrontegui
Cookery consultant: Maria Esperanza Fuguep
Cooking assistants: Luca Pagliari and Oriol Roset
Texts: Xim Fuster and Manel Gómez
Photography: Oriol Aleu

First edition in the Spanish language 2005

© 2005, Xim fuster, Manel Gómez for the texts
© 2005, Oriol Aleu for the photographs

ISBN: 84-8478-188-7
Legal record: B-49120-2005

Typeset, printed and bound at:
Aleu, S.A.
Llull 48-52, Barcelona

Translation: Natalia Ferrer, Madeleine Cases and Gean Silverstone

t is no easy task to describe the ancestral alchemy secrets of a people. It is difficult to move among ancient fires and gas rings, close to cooks proud of their lore, and unveil procedures that have survived only by word-of-mouth. Fishermen and farmers tend to be hermetic when asked to disclose the secrets of their captures at sea and harvests on land. Nevertheless, we here attempt to disclose some information, not extensive but rigorous, as to what Minorca offers. This is an island defined and enriched by a wealth of peoples who have left behind a special identity in all domains, including the field of gastronomy.

This book will tell you about food consumed in the past and food eaten at present on the island, dishes surprisingly well conserved with the passing of time. You will delight in carefully captured images which – even for those who are not food lovers – will tempt you to find out more about Minorca's gastronomic culture.

In this work, Triangle Postals presents a panoply of elements, from traditions and habits to specific recipes. Cheese, cold meats, calderetas, gin, crespells… you will see. See the variety and wealth of aromas and flavours emanating from this land, taste them, taste the land, and – why not – experiment. We are sure you will be delighted.

Bon appetit.

The authors

Millenary land

Minorca is the easternmost island of the Balearics and has a wealth of culture in its past. The different dominations suffered throughout centuries have enriched the land and its peoples with traditions and habits going well beyond the Mediterranean. It is not surprising, then, that the different folk who lived on the island left behind a beneficial inheritance. This fact, together with the island's peculiar geography, have shaped Minorcan peoples' characters and their everyday lives.

Some 4,000 years ago, during the pre-Talayotic age, Minorca was populated for the first time. A second wave of people came around 1400 BC, and this ensued in the development of the Talayotic culture. Up to 123 BC, the time in which the Roman Empire came, the island was inhabited successively by Phoenicians, Greeks and Carthaginians, who found this place an interesting location on the way of their trading routes throughout the Mediterranean.

Roman domination went on until the year 902 and was to leave the greatest imprint of those times. After repeated vandal plundering and looting, the Muslim peoples invaded Minorca, and that meant a new way of life for the Minorcan peoples, who went on to be dependants of the Cordovan Caliphate.

On January 17th 1287 the Catalan troops conquered the island, which afterwards would remain Christian. The Crown of Aragon disembarked in the Maó harbour lead by King Alphonse III. A short time after that the Muslims still hiding in the Saint Agueda castle in Ferreries deposed arms and surrendered.

Later on, in times of the kingdoms of Charles I and Phillip II, the territory experienced times of hardship because of the frequent lootings carried out by the Turks in the Mediterranean. The Turks had increased their power as a naval force. After that, the year in which the famous Redbeard disembarked, 1535, is known as "the year of misfortune", because of the destruction and havoc this pirate left in his wake as he ravaged the area of Ciutadella.

The greatest splendour came in the 18th century, when Minorca went on to belong, no less than three times, to the British, as well as undergoing a brief French domination spell. With the signing of the Amiens Treaty in 1802, the island became part of the Spanish Crown once and for all.

The surface of Minorca is of 701.84 square kilometres with 216 kilometres of coast, and the territory is divided into eight municipalities: Maó (the administrative capital), Ciutadella, Alaior, es Castell, Ferreries, es Mercadal, Sant Lluís and es Mitjorn Gran. This last village acquired municipal independence at the end of the 20th century.

Minorca is frequently defined as very flat territory, as its highest point, el Toro, has an altitude of

Minorca's climate is Mediterranean. It is characterized by moderate temperatures, little rain and considerable humidity as well as strong north winds.

The Minorca coastline is 216 kilometres long. It has a varied relief as the north lies on different geological sediments from the south.

358 metres. However, its relief is varied indeed, the reason for that being its geological composition: the Northern section of the island lies on a layer of diverse materials from the Primary, Secondary and Quaternary Eras and presents a rugged coastline. The South, though, is made up of a Tertiary limestone platform, full of ravines and abundant vegetation, and here the land ends in gentle beaches of the finest white sand. Maó harbour is a natural formation and it is considered one of the safest throughout the Mediterranean.

The climate is typically Mediterranean, that is, gentle temperatures around an annual average between 16.5 and 17.5 degrees Centigrade, about 2,452 sunshine hours and moderate rainfall, 600 litres per square metre is the average. Another feature, shared by neighbouring islands, is the prevailing humidity, up to an annual average of 69%. The prevailing wind is the well-known tramontana, blowing from the North, cold and dry in nature. Sometimes wind episodes – locally known as *tramuntanades* – will blow at speeds of more than 100km per hour.

In 1993 the island territory was declared Reserve of the Biosphere by UNESCO, because of its ability to harmonize economic and social development together with the preservation of the environment. This indeed is a commitment Minorcan people agreed to share in enthusiastically, for their own benefit and that of future generations.

For centuries Minorca's inhabitants have defended environmental preservation and have been engaged in sustainable development. Thus UNESCO has recognized the island as a reserve of the biosphere.

The nuances
of gastronomy

Owing to the varied nature of influences occurring in the territory, both because of climate and geographical factors and historical and economic vicissitudes, Minorcan cuisine is difficult to summarize with one single predominant flavour. A first approximation to culinary identity comes, not from books, but rather from oral tradition, which incorporated variations whilst keeping stomachs satisfied.

However, and as is the case everywhere, Minorcan cuisine has always relied on the crops and catches coming from its land and its sea. Bearing in mind the geographical context, Minorca has used olive oil, wine, pulses and foods in brine – all typical features of Mediterranean cuisine, with some Arabian remnants contributing to its substrates -, in contrast to the ingredients and procedures used in other European cultures.

Minorca also learned from other cultures, because of the 18th century dominations, and it was enriched by the British and French contributions, among others. It should be added that, because of frequent times of hardship, imagination came to the fore more than once in order to enjoy tasty dishes, however humble. This is what is generically referred to as "subsistence cooking". It is not exclusive to Minorca, but Minorca has known how to make it productive. This is so much the case that nowadays, in times of plenty, "poor cuisine" has become quite distinctive and well-known for its simplicity and good taste.

And, of course, the sea and the coastline – elements inextricably linked to an island – have meant a fabulous contribution of produce helping towards the definition of this gastronomic personality.

Despite the fact that nowadays any product is available to us all year round, regardless of the time of the year, the fact is that natural cycles, seasons and important dates coincide with today's cuisine, yet another of tradition's legacies.

In the references chapter, we must highlight an essential work which shows us the folklore and contributes strikingly to gastronomic culture. This is the book "De re cibaria", by Pere Ballester, printed in 1923. Little had been published in the field before, only some references coming from the Archduke Louis Salvador in 1891, referring to common culinary uses but not giving any recipe. These texts in turn looked for sources in anonymous manuscripts or very humble publications, the only available recipe books which required great creativity on behalf of the readers to be able to cook successfully.

British recipes, French influence, Arab substrates…
Mediterranean and Anglo-Saxon practices
converge in the making of certain dishes.

Nowadays native species such as the Minorcan hen and cow enjoy a special protection policy, although in the past their number dwindled notably.

Tools for good eating

The diversity of cultures experienced by Minorca throughout the centuries has made it possible for its cuisine to take good advantage. In the case of Arabian influences, *cuscussó* and *arrós de la terra* are there to tell the tale; of the British, Minorcan cuisine maintains a preference for cooking with butter rather than lard; sweet and savoury puddings, and also some English words. From the French, mayonnaise was kept (and in fact its name stems from the town of Maó) and went on to become internationally famous.

Vegetables and garden produce are the basis for most of the dishes cooked, in which we frequently observe the presence of fish, shell-fish, meat, pasta... A quick review of ways of cooking is a good example: *oliaigües*, shell-fish and fish stews or *calderes*, *panaderes*, dry rice and rice in sauce, *perol al forn*, garnishment and some preserves that are then used as a base.

The procedures are also important. *Oliaiqua*, for example, can be prepared in many ways. The base consists of oil, garlic, water and bread, and to that one may add tomato, green pepper and onion, sometimes figs, and even cabbage, asparagus or eggs.

The *caldera* is not only lobster caldera. The essence of this dish is to be found in its elaboration, not the basic ingredient. The basis consists of fried vegetables and fish; or maybe done the fishermen's way, directly boiling all the ingredients in water. The *panadera* also consists of a base of fried tomato and vegetables, but it may be made of meat or fish, and the common element in most is potato. Rice is another basic ingredient, combining with practically everything: vegetables, pulses, fish and meat and even cold meats, mushrooms, poultry and different broths that may vary in consistency.

The *perol* owes its name to the recipient used for cooking, which can be made of clay, glass or metal. The main feature of the dish is the cooking procedure, always in the oven. The main ingredients are meat, fish or vegetables that may be stuffed, accompanied by a potato base or other produce.

Baking deserves a special mention, as in Minorca sweet and savoury are often mixed, from the most basic dish as is the case of cheese with grapes, to the sobrassada coca, made of a cold meat variant, sobrassada, which goes really well with sweet flavours.

Cold meats, cheese and dry nuts add their characteristic flair to Minorcan cuisine; all of them are often present in a number of recipes, and are sometimes difficult to accept by other palates.

Sea and land give the ingredients used in the Minorcan cuisine. The methods used are the other important part of the personality of the local gastronomy.

ANA ELISA
3ºMH1-501

From the sea
and the coast

Being an island, Minorca has always lived in close contact with the sea, making it possible to obtain an extensive diversity of sea foods. Fish, seafoods and crustaceans or molluscs represent a sizeable proportion of the ingredients used in Minorcan cooking. This produce is not only the defining identity of Mediterranean cuisine, but also contributes protein and minerals bringing their nutrient value to a level similar to that found in meat, milk or eggs.

As happens elsewhere, there is "white" and "blue" fish in Minorca, and the classification depends on the fat content of each species. Thus, white fish such as monkfish and hake present white muscle flesh and a shiny hue clearly conveying the lean nature of the flesh, which has less than 4 per cent fat. On the other hand, blue fish bears a reddish tone with greater fat contents in percentages over 5 per cent that may even go up to 25 or 30 per cent. Mackerel, horse mackerel and sardine, for example, are species

As an island, its contact with the sea enabled Minorca to enjoy a large variety of produce from the sea: fish, seafood, crustacea and molluscs are regular ingredients.

belonging to this group, with fatty deposits enabling them to resist the long migration routes they follow.

Sea foods are eaten in many different ways: in soup, rice, *panaderes*, cakes and puddings; also fried, grilled, boiled or baked. These are indeed some of the dishes and techniques that tend to appear in traditional cookery books.

A good suggestion for brilliant cooking results is to go to the market early in the morning and buy fresh fish. In Minorca fresh fish is easy to find, as there are fishmongers close to the fishing source areas. We should add that fishing as a profession has been actively maintained, and the professional fishing fleet is fully and regularly active.

Much variety can be found at the market. Fish is ever-present in the stalls, and according to the season we find red mullet, bream, cathead, parrot fish, sargo, scorpion fish, grouper, red snapper, sardine, squid, cuttlefish, octopus, lobster, crayfish, shrimp, embossed clam, date shell, Noah's ark, mussel… The way to prepare each one is generally linked to the ingredient itself.

The *caldera* or soup dish is the best-known Minorcan dish, and the most representative is lobster *caldereta*. The season for lobster goes from the month of March to the end of August, when lobster fishing is legally forbidden in order to allow for natural restocking. All rice dishes cooked in stock use fish or shell-fish as the main ingredient, and the end result is much appreciated.

The oven is another means of obtaining delicious dishes. Fish is well suited to oven baking, also shellfish and molluscs. Stuffed squid baked in the oven is an essential recipe in all the island's cookery books, and its high acclaim is due to the very subtle flavour nuances experienced by the palate.

With the tourist boom, the diversity of seafood dishes made gastronomy another attraction to add to the list of what Minorca has to offer. Good proof of this is the proliferation of fish restaurants and eateries to be found, especially in the three main harbours (Maó, Ciutadella and Fornells).

Another factor contributing to the island's own cookbook is the fact that many Minorcan families, then and now, own a small boat – good for fishing at the week-end and especially in summer. This made it possible for a direct relationship to develop between produce and consumers. In the summer it was a tradition to sail around the island at least once, and this is something still done today. On these trips, the sailors would be obliged to survive on the fish they caught themselves. Armed with the somewhat limited tackle and gear carried on board, and using whatever catch had been made, these family sailors had to devise all sorts of tricks and ideas in order not to get bored with their cooking, with their cooking, thus giving rise to a variety of ways of preparing fish.

Fishing, either professional or amateur, has been a basic element in the creation of recipes of Minorcan traditional cuisine.

3-MH-1-492

The fruits
of the earth

Minorca has maintained its agricultural activity as yet another part of its economy, even in present times, and this has made it possible for the island to count on fresh local produce at all times. Crops represent approximately 51 per cent of Minorca's territory, and all agricultural activities are regulated directly by the agricultural and farming sector.

One of the most popular crops is potato, although the seeds must be imported from outside the island. Both the white and red skinned varieties are consumed in Minorca. There existed an indigenous potato variety, small and reddish, that nowadays has practically disappeared.

Tomato is very much present in many regularly consumed dishes. Other than the better-known tomatoes consumed in salad, it is also normal to see *tomàtics de penjar* (hanging tomatoes), which are preserved by hanging after being tied together using string. We can also consume *tomàtic de ramellet* (bunch of tomatoes on a branch), good for making *pa amb oli* (bread with rubbed tomato) and also *oliaigua*. Both in tomato sauces used as a base for other preparations and also in salads we can find onions, green pepper, red pepper and garlic. We should point out that not all of these vegetables are grown in Minorca.

Lettuce is used for salads. The most popular type of lettuce is romaine lettuce or cos, which, different to others, is big in size, with long leaves and a strong taste.

The main aubergine variety in Minorca is very white inside and its skin is dark purple; it can only be found fresh during the summer season, as it is impossible to grow in a hothouse where pollination would not occur.

There is an indigenous artichoke variety, slightly elongated and narrower at one end, of a purple hue. It can be used for casseroles and *panaderes*, and is also very good for frying in batter. Courgettes can also be prepared in many ways: stuffed, baked or fried in thin slices served to accompany the main dish. Fruit varieties grown on the island are fully Mediterranean. Pippin is the most appreciated type of apple, as it is of a medium size and slightly flat, very good for cooking purposes. We also find the Kane variety, brought to the island by the British in the 18th century. Kane apples are not easily found at market stalls, but can be at a number of farms. Figs are also very popular in Minorca, owing to their very sweet red and white pulp. They can be eaten raw on their own, accompanying an *oliaigua* dish, cooked or in preserve. Pears are typically eaten fresh, and the most popular variety is the St. John pear, with green skin sometimes specked with brown, small in size and very tasty, acid, with a firm pulp. Its name defines its season, at the beginning of summer. Yellow melon (honeydew melon) is the best known in Minorca, very much appreciated for its sweetness; there is also a hedgehog melon, a variety indigenous to the Balearic Islands.

In the local markets we find tomatoes, lettuce, aubergines and artichokes as well as other Mediterranean vegetables.

Pulses are also important in Minorcan cuisine. Broad beans, lentils, beans, *guixons* (small beans very much used in the island) and chick-peas, amongst others, can be prepared in thousands of different ways.

Olives, and olive oil of course, are key in Minorcan cuisine. Although the island's olive groves are not grown for crops anymore, olive trees were part and parcel of Minorcan farming. Olive oil consumption has not decreased and is widely used, for example, in sweet pastry, amongst other cooking uses. Olive trees grew by the hundreds only a few decades ago, and the olive tree scion would be grafted onto a wild olive tree in order to achieve good production of a fruit earlier than the common olive.

Other produce can also be found at the market stalls, but they are better considered if obtained directly from the soil. A deeply rooted tradition is that of asparagus, snail and mushroom picking, obviously dependent on the season. The most popular mushrooms are lactarius, king trumpet and chanterelle, usually eaten together with meat dishes, although they are delicious as well when *sauté* or grilled on their own. Snails are usually boiled with herbs and other aromatic ingredients; they come to the table together with *alioli* sauce and boiled potatoes, or also cooked in a stew with spider crab. And finally, asparagus go well with *oliaigua, panadera* and omelette.

Fur and feather

Meat consumption is frequently made to depend on cattle-raising and hunting practices. Pork, veal and lamb are the meats most used in the traditional cookbook, although we could also add chicken and rabbit to the list. Pig is the animal from which almost everything is used, both because of traditional cold meat and sausage production and also because it is an easy animal to raise and fatten. Cows are used both for milk and meat consumption. There are two different cattle species on the island: the red Minorcan cow, an indigenous milk-producing breed in Spain; and the Friesian cow, genetically improved, constituting most of the cow population on the island. Let us mention two other indigenous species: the Minorcan sheep and the Minorcan hen, both still raised in Minorca although their consumption is not all that extended.

Hunting is an activity limited by official close seasons and the scarcity of some species. Animals hunted most are: quail, partridge, thrush, wood pigeon, woodcock and rabbit. Using guns and taking dogs along, hunting techniques on the island include animal capture with *filat en coll* (lasso) and taking male partridges as a decoy. In fact, bird hunting using *filat en coll* is characteristic of Minorca: the technique consists of setting a net by tying it to two branches, in the shape of an open fan. The net is placed in sites visited by the birds at dawn and dusk.

Farming and agriculture are present in more than 50% of the
territory. The Minorcan cuisine is embellished with the variety
of local produce given by the land.

Specialties of the house

As well as producing high quality ingredients, Minorca is the home ground for brands that are famous well beyond its borders, as with the case of Maó-Minorca cheese ("Mahón Cheese"), distinguished with a Designation of Origin certificate. Among the cold meats produced, *sobrassada* is well-known abroad and is stored in many of the island's pantries. We should also mention gin as a representative element of the region's gastronomy. There are many other foods under the "Balearic Produce" stamp which offer the highest quality, such as gin itself or the island's "Illa de Menorca" wine. Other products manufactured by a number of local companies also bear the same distinction. We could mention honey, lamb, sweet pastry, artisan cold meats, chocolate, liqueurs and even ostrich meat.

specialties of the house

Maó-Minorca cheese

The protected Designation of Origin products are closely linked to the geographical region they come from. In the case of Maó-Minorca cheese, geographical and climate factors such as soil features, temperature, humidity, light, together with human intervention in the manufacturing process and traditional maturing practices have all combined to render very specific features in aroma and flavour to the final product.

There are documents from the 5th century already mentioning the consumption of cheese in Minorca, and Arabic texts from the year 1000 praising the cheese's excellence. Further on, during the 13th century, the amounts of cheese exported were quite considerable, and the exporting activity increased under British rule. Indeed, the original shipping harbour, Maó (Mahón) gave its name to the product.

Cheese was and still is the main source of income for Minorca farmers. At the end of the 20th century there were hundreds of cattle farms working on cheese either for direct consumption or for indirect consumption through agrarian cooperative groups created years ago and still active.

Maó cheese is made from cow's milk and is the only Designation of Origin cheese of the Balearic Islands. It is also one of the few DOP cheese in Spain

to be made using only cow's milk. A Regulating Board has been acting since 1985 which guarantees the high quality of the organic features of this product. Maó cheese comes in three varieties: semi hard, with a distinct orange hue to the rind; dense, with small holes and a buttery texture making it easy to slice; and hard, presenting a firm and hard texture. The latter can also come in a vintage version when left to mature for longer. In this case, the texture becomes flaky, flavour intensifies and the taste stays longer, making this variety the one gourmets appreciate the most. Combined with grapes, vintage hard cheese becomes a surprising delicacy.

Diversity of flavour is, then, the second defining

Mahon cheeses have a characteristic orange colour and a
square shape with rounded edges.

feature of Maó cheese. This versatility makes it possible to use Maó cheese in a number of preparations and salads or simply eat it with bread, tomato and oil. Cheese is also used in baking and pastry, and it is typical to serve cheese as an appetizer before meals, together with olives and other local produce.

As the semi hard cheese melts beautifully (its texture is smooth and creamy), this cheese is good for many dishes *au gratin* (pasta and potatoes, for instance) and also for bringing aroma to sweet and savoury flour doughs. Some restaurants even make cheese ice-cream with Maó cheese as the main ingredient.

The square shape is yet another distinctive trait, and this peculiar shape of the cheese is a direct result of the way in which cheese is manufactured. The correct amount of curdled milk is separated by using a special cheesecloth called *fogasser*, which eventually produces the square shape.

And finally, Maó cheese had always been manufactured in farmhouses following the traditional procedure, using fresh cow's milk (mainly from Friesian cows, although Minorca and the originally Swiss Alpine brown cows are also used). This traditional practice still continues in some areas, using old techniques passed on from generation to generation. Raw milk may eventually be mixed with 5 per cent Minorca sheep's milk.

gastronomy_**minorca**

Once the milk has curdled it divides into separate grains, the curds. In order to curdle the milk, rennet must be used, and in Minorca the agent used was, traditionally, wild thistle pistils. The rennet agent must be left in for about 45 minutes to one hour, at 32-33 degrees Centigrade, and after this the mass is transferred to a special recipient that separates the curds.

After curdling, the mass will separate into curds and whey (called *xerigot* or *serum*), the latter being the liquid part of the milk separated from the solid curds. Although not used for cheese-making, it does have other applications. Whey is extracted from the vat by opening a tap which transfers the liquid to another container, after which everything has to be washed in abundant water.

After some time, the curd is separated and made into one solid shape by means of the special cheesecloth, the *fogasser*. The solid mass is made into a ball, all by

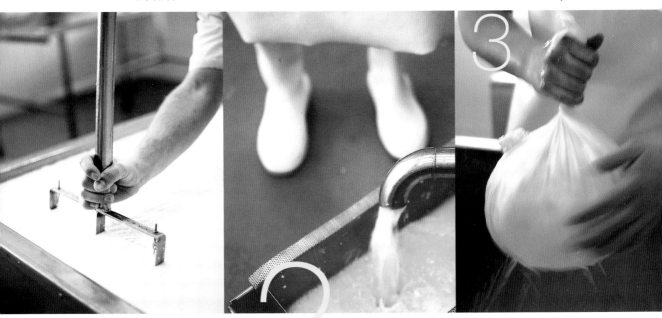

hand, making sure similar amounts are taken for each cheese. This process will fix the final weight of the product when it goes to market.

How is cheese made?

Once well wrapped up, the pre-moulding and pressing process is carried out by hand in order to express the remaining whey. In the old days, when cheese was made in farmhouses the traditional way, farmers were so adept at this that they were able to hold the four

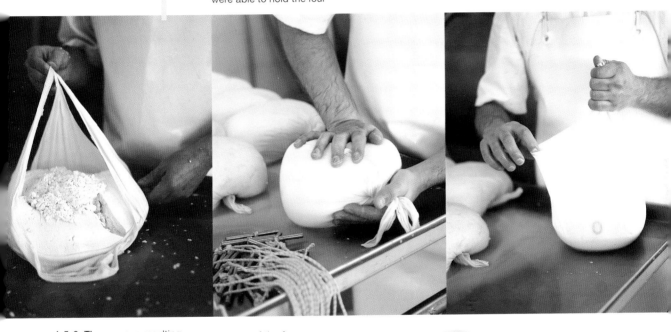

4-5-6. **The process** resulting in the final shape of the cheese requires patience, as the mass must set gradually adapting to the fine gauze mould. The *fogasser* is placed on a wide, flat surface called cheesing table or *taula de formatjar*, and is used to wrap up the curdled milk; with one hand the cheesecloth is lifted by its four corners in order to compress the mass.

corners of the *fogasser* cheesecloth by their teeth while turning the piece with their hands in order to leave it ready for tying.

The *lligam* is the special string used to tie and close the *fogasser*. The string must not be too fine, as it will have to tie the cheese tight for pre-pressing. As can be seen, the string takes the four corners of the cheesecloth and closes the cheese. This operation requires experience.

Pressing is the process that will finally give Minorcan cheese its characteristic shape, typically square.

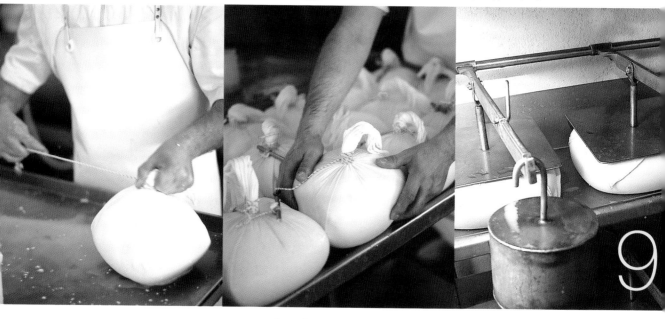

Once the moulding process has been completed with each one of the cheese, and once they are all well tied, they are left to lie on one same tray, ready for the final pressing. The *lligam* string straps each parcel extremely tight, closing any opening with a knot. All cheeses stay on the cheesing table, ready for the pressing procedure.

Pressing is intense and lasts between two and three hours.

Salting is the next stage. The cheese are tumbled straight into a bath of salt solution called *salmorra* (brine) or *aigua-sal*, at a temperature between 10 and 15 degrees Centigrade. This brine-immersion process lasts for one to two days. After salting, the

Ripening is the slowest process. After one month (in the old days the cheese would be put on reed mats for airing to be optimal), the rind is greased – that is, covered either in cow's milk butter or pure olive oil and

Upon withdrawing the cheeses, once pressing is over, a special design called *mamella* (small breast) is embossed on the cheese by exerting pressure on the folds of the cheesecloth and the knots of the piece. Although the *fogassa* is formed, the cheese is a long way from being a finished product yet.

fogasses or cheese pieces are taken out of the liquid and turned regularly for every side to be adequately aired. Mould must be avoided at all costs. If a cheese gets mouldy, however, it will be carefully cleaned making sure the cheese as such remains intact.

paprika. The time to maturing will change according to the variety intended. Semi-hard cheese takes around two months. Once the process is completed, the rind will have turned smooth and unctuous, slightly yellow or orange in colour. The cheese inside, however, is easy to cut and not elastic, with different-sized holes that tend to be smaller than a pea in size.

THE VARIETIES

The colour of Maó cheese is different according to the degree of ripening. When soft, the colour is close to white. As time goes by, the older the rind the darker it will become, actually coming close to very dark. The typical colour of Minorcan cheese is of an orange hue, both in the semi-hard and hard varieties, which are the ones most sold. Taste will also vary according to maturation. In any case, the Maó-Minorca cheese is one of the best-liked Designations of Origin in Spain, because of its versatility and possible uses in all kinds of cooking. The export figures are good proof of the cheese's popularity everywhere.

Soft. Three weeks to two months' ripening. Tastes slightly salty, smooth, milky and a bit acid, and may evoke the flavour of fresh curd. The characteristic colour of this variety is ivory white.

Semi-hard. The best-known and widest sold variety outside the island. The taste is stronger, saltier, and its texture is that of a slightly buttery paste to the palate. Holes are small and the cheese is easily sliced. The rind presents an orange hue.

Hard. This is the variety most recently acknowledged by the Regulatory Board of Designation of Origin. The texture of the cheese is firm and hard, with an intense flavour to the palate. The paste is dry, yellow, and slightly hot in taste

Very hard. The one most favoured by gourmets and which requires at least five months' ripening. The rind is brown and the inside flakes easily. The taste is very intense and long-lasting in the mouth

2

1

3

4

Pork, a wealth of meat

As is the case of many other regions, the pig is one of the farm animals offering the broadest range of meat products after processing. Other than cooking with pork, Minorcan cold meats are very much appreciated throughout the Mediterranean. There are many cold meats to choose from; some denominations are shared with the island of Majorca, and others are exclusive to Minorca. A standard classification for cold meats establishes a number of categories: fresh, raw, cured, scalded and boiled.

Sobrassada, carn i xulla, botifarró (black and

white) and *calmot* (*camallot* or cuixot) are the best-known varieties, especially *sobrassada*, which is made throughout the Balearic Islands. *Sobrassada* is a fermented cold meat; that is, made from dried-out raw meat – the transformations that take place during the process are due to microbial flora which give characteristic taste and aroma. There are different *sobrassada* varieties, such as *sobrassada vella* (old) and poltrú, made using thicker gut (the cecum, the bladder…) which confers different size and shape to the piece.

However, *carn i xulla* is made only in Minorca, and it may well be the most ancient pork preparation manufactured on the island. It is also raw sausage, although in this case cured rather than fermented. The product, made by mincing lean meat and bacon and then adding spices and salt, can probably be traced back to Roman charcuterie. The manufacturing process includes drying out the meat inside the intestine, at the same time as other tasks of elaboration are carried out.

The Minorcan *camot* is special in that the mince mix produces a smaller granulation to the *camot* made in Majorca. As is the case of *carn xulla* and *camot*, the black and white varieties of *botifarrons* (thick sausage) come to us from Roman times.

Practically all the meat of the pig is used. The most characteristic sausages and cold meats come from the Roman period and are *Carn i xulla, camot* and *butifarrons*

1

The cutting of the meat is the first step for the preparation of the raw material to be processed. In Minorca, pig slaughters are called *porquejades*, and the traditional time for the killing of the pig is in winter, the best season for adequate curing the cold meats and ensuring better preservation.

All the pig's entrails and pieces of meat are meticulously cut and prepared for consumption. Each organ is the focus of well defined gastronomic goals, and that is the reason why all parts must be previously separated. In the case of *sobrassada*, this cured cold meat is made, as already we know, using both lean meat and bacon, and two varieties are known: tender and cured.

3

The careful mincing of lean meat and bacon is the first step towards making *sobrassada*. Once the lean meat and the bacon have been selected and cleaned

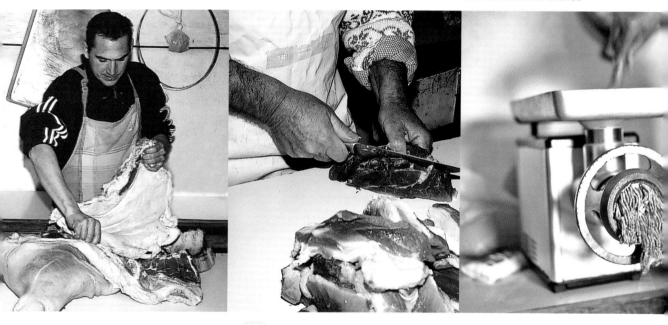

2

in order to be mixed with the other ingredients, they are minced together in varying proportions; sometimes there will be more meat and others more bacon in the mix. The size of the meat granules obtained in the mix is less than 6 millimetres in diameter.

Pork products

The mixing procedure involves combining the mince together with spices and other ingredients. We should point out that, by mincing, the muscular structure of the meat has been well fragmented, and this will ensure an optimal mix of the ingredients that make up the *sobrassada*. The temperature throughout this process must be kept between 2 and 5 degrees Celsius.

The process is carried out by hand, and the aim of such mixing is to guarantee a smooth paste – and this would not be possible by simply adding the new ingredients during the meat and bacon mincing process. At this stage we add sweet paprika – sometimes hot paprika too – (between 4 and 7 per cent) and salt (between 1.8 and 2.8 per cent).

The **packing** of the paste is the process by which the mixed paste is stuffed into the gut, and according to the type of gut used a different product will be obtained, both in name and aspect. In Minorca, for example, we have tender and cured *sobrassada*. The tender variety is stuffed into intestines that are very thin and curved into an elongated "U" shape. The ends are tied with twine which will be used for hanging the piece. The taste of the tender variety is smooth and balanced, and the colour is a very deep red. However, the cured *sobrassada* is made by stuffing the mixture into thicker gut and it requires a longer time for maturation. The taste is stronger and the colour is darker red.

There are other products, such as *poltrú*, that use the cecum part of the gut, the bladder – as we can see in the image – or other parts and materials for stuffing. The end resull is that of larger and rounder pieces, and the time of maturation is longer. The resulting flavour will be even stronger, drier, although the essence is basically similar in the different varieties.

The tying of the twine closes the aperture of the gut. The twine's function is to isolate the mass – the filling – from agents that might be harmful to the meat; and it is also used for hanging the piece during maturation and curing.

The gut – whether natural or

When tying the twine, one must pull downward after the knot in order to go round all the gut or bladder, taking considerable care to achieve the right shape and firmness to the product; which is how the characteristic oval shape is attained.

The tying procedure obviously changes from one variety to another. Thus, tender *sobrassada* is tied at both ends, and cured *sobrassada*, thicker, is sometimes tied only at one end.

During maturation paprika is rubbed onto the tip of the knot, and this ensures the cold meat's protection as far as external agents are concerned. Tender *sobrassada* requires 5 to

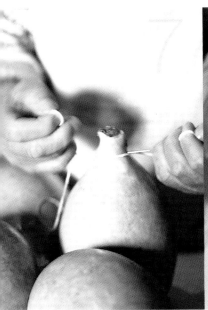

man-made – is always cleaned and washed meticulously in order to eliminate any possible remains and debris. The washing procedure also contributes to effective maturation, because a moist gut gains in elasticity, and this in turn ensures the absence of air pockets inside.

6 days before it can be put on sale, and it weighs close on to 300 grams. Cured *sobrassada* requires approximately four months for full maturation, and it weighs 800 grams. Poltrú and other varieties may be larger and that calls for a longer maturation time.

Herbs and spices used

Every cold meat and sausage variety contains a number of spices which give a specific and very characteristic taste. It has to be said that in Minorca the number of herbs and spices used in the making of cold meats is rather scant. The main ingredients used are black pepper, sweet paprika, hot paprika, white pepper, aniseed, cinnamon and salt. However, herbs such as rosemary, thyme and oregano are used occasionally, depending on the tastes and preferences of each producer.

Having said this, though, it does not follow that a limited number of ingredients means that a product is poor in variety, as can easily be tested.

Sobrassada. The best known pork product, as it shares its name and fame with Majorca and Ibiza. The fermentation of the meat, cured with spices, is one of its defining traits. Delicious with bread

Carn i xulla. A cold meat product typical and exclusive to Minorca, although it probably owes its origin to charcuterie in times of Roman domination.

Camot. Also known as cuixot in the area of Ciutadella, it consists of minced meat mixed with blood and black pepper, paprika and aniseed. The meat is not stuffed in gut, but in the skin of the pig's leg (thus the name in Minorca refers in both cases to the hind quarters of the animal).

Botifarró blanc, whiter in appearance than the botifarró negre, as the mix in this case does not add blood. It includes other parts of the pig and it is stuffed into thin membrane. Usually eaten fried or grilled.

Botifarró negre is made using the same ingredients and spices as the *camot*. It is stuffed into the small intestine, tying the mix into sausages on a string, and it can be eaten raw or cooked.

Gin, the British legacy

Gin probably originated in the North of Europe, possibly in Holland, and it was introduced in Minorca thanks to the British rules that took place throughout the 18th century. Even at present, the gin produced in Minorca is manufactured the traditional way, in old copper stills heated up directly by wood fires. The distillation process uses wine alcohol – and not alcohol from cereal as in the original formula – and is aromatized with juniper berries (the fruit must be imported from neighbouring countries, as optimal crops are obtained at an altitude of 800 to 1,000 metres) and other herbs – secret to each manufacturer – which result in the characteristic taste to this very aromatic gin. The distilled liquid is stored in oak barrels cured with gin for the gin not to colour. The alcohol content is between 30 and 43 per cent, and the final product is acknowledged with the Designation of Origin stamp. Artificial extracts or additives are not allowed.

This drink is undoubtedly part and parcel of the gastronomic identity of the island. Its consumption is closely linked to Minorca's annual festivals and celebrations. *Pomada* – gin mixed with lemon juice – is served cold, usually mixed on a basis of two parts of lemon to one of gin. Another typical beverage is *pellofa*, gin aromatized with lemon peel and a squirt of soda. Of course, gin can always be taken straight, served in a small glass, or on the rocks.

The juniper berry is the characteristic fruit of Minorcan gin, a geographical denomination that shows the importance of this drink specially linked to the local fiestas and to the *pomada* (Minorcan gin with lemonade).

Made with flour

Flour is the main ingredient for a wealth of products. Bread is the best known, but there is a whole range of varieties that in the past were closely related to the calendar and now constitute a gastronomic universe which is greatly appreciated throughout the island. The dough is often used to wrap up fillings, or comes as an accompaniment to local produce. This is the case of the *rubiol*, made of meat, fish or vegetables; the *flaó*, savoury dough mixed with cheese; the *agulles* and *croissants* made with *sobrassada*…

Among so many varieties, we would like to focus on *formatjada*, both because of its personality and its deep-rooted popularity. The dough consists of flour and lard, and it wraps up fillings generally made of a mix of different meats (*sobrassada*, meat, bacon…). In the same way as the *flaó*, the *crespells* and other pastries, *formatjada* is typically consumed by the islanders in the Easter period.

Coca is yet another popular savoury product, especially because of its versatility, as the dough is usually a rectangular base which is covered with a number of different ingredients. The dough is made with soft flour, oil, lard, water, yeast and sometimes egg. It can be served covered or uncovered. The filling varies, because the base will allow practically any ingredient. The most traditional are *coques* made of vegetables, tomato sauce, and peppers, although others may contain fish and meat.

Flour is a universal base in alimentation. From bread to sophisticated preparations, there is an important baking tradition in Minorca.

Wheat flour and yeast are the main ingredients of bread. The *panes de payés* are big, round bread loaves, very low in salt or with none at all and with a firm, dense crumb. These large bread loaves last more than a day, enough for the whole family. There are loaves that can weigh up to three kilos.

It must be said that bread, as a gastronomic procedure linked to subsistence cooking, is all used up, even when hard, as long as no mould has formed. In this case, the piece of bread is cut finely and the slices are used in different dishes such as *oliaigua, panaderes* and fish *calderes*, among others. Mixed with milk, hard bread is good for making puddings.

OVEN SPECIALITIES

4. Vegetable *rubiols*. Different from the other type, these are usually filled with spinach, and sometimes have pine nuts and raisins added.

5. *Flaó.* Round shaped pastry filled with cheese and egg – baking makes it rise and eventually fill out to take on its traditional rounded shape.

6. Vegetable *coca*. Made in a llauna or *perol* (wide flat baking tray), it has a rectangular shape. It can be covered with just about any ingredients: tomato and vegetable sauce, vegetables, fish, meat…

7. *Formatjada.* Traditional Minorcan pie baked in a shape specially for holding other ingredients within, typically pork, bacon and *sobrassada*. It is traditionally eaten during the Easter season.

8. *Coca* with *sobrassada*. Using the dough for sweet pastry coca, with sugar sprinkled on top, *sobrassada* becomes particularly tasty.

9. Covered *coca*. With the same ingredients as the *rubiol*, although instead of making small pastries the dough is baked and shaped into one single piece that will later on be cut into slices.

1. Filled *croissant*. Although this pastry is from elsewhere, in Minorca the custom is to fill it with local produce, such as *sobrassada* or Maó cheese.

2. *Agulla de sobrassada* (*sobrassada* needle). Small pastry eaten between meals or as an appetizer. The "needle" is filled with *sobrassada*.

3. Meat or fish *rubiol*. Made of fine flour, oil, lard and egg and filled with fish, meat, tomato sauce, onion and other ingredients. *Rubiols* are traditional pastry of the Balearic Islands.

Pastries, cakes and more sweets

Cakes and baking are very popular in Minorca. And this is only logical if you happen to see the incredible amount and diversity of products baked on the island: *amargos, carquinyols, pastissets, crespellines, crespells* (filled with marmalade, sweet potato, *suquet*, cottage cheese and sweet shredded pumpkin, amongst other ingredients), *coques bambes*, oil and sugar *coca*, fruit *coca* (apricot, cherries), *coques amb roes, congrets, ensaimadas* (that come with a number of different fillings), puff pastries, *orellanes* (pronounced as "oranes"), *dolces*...

Cakes and tarts with whipped cream and meringue are specialties of the island, and the two most popular may well be the *amargos* and *carquinyols*. *Amargos* consist of ground almond, white sugar and egg well mixed together to make a biscuit shape which is baked for firmness and consistency. The *carquinyols*, however, are smaller in size, square in shape and dry, although they are made with the same ingredients as the *amargos*, adding flour for a more solid texture.

Dolces are also very typical. These are elongated sugar sponge pastries usually eaten at annual festivals and celebrations, taken with water and aniseed. They are made in different colours (pink, white, yellow, green...).

Despite its name, the *"amargo"* (bitter), made of ground almonds, white sugar and egg, is very sweet and is much appreciated when eaten between meals.

Meringue alone, baked in the oven, is also a much appreciated sweet.

Meringue. This is quite a simple sweet to prepare, and it is used for filling and covering a number of cakes and pastries. Well-whisked frothy egg white is the main ingredient. In a pan with hot water we add as many *unces* (every *unça* equals approximately 33 grams) of sugar as egg whites whisked. When the syrup is done, just before it turns into caramel, it is poured over the whisked egg whites. This must be done stirring constantly till all the liquid has been poured. The end result can be eaten as it is or baked for a different texture.

Meringues can be aromatized with a number of natural ingredients, such as lemon, cinnamon, coffee, strawberry…

Meringue is one of the main preparations in Minorcan pastry-making. It is used as filling, coating or alone when well seasoned.

Tortada and brazo de gitano. Meringue is used in many sweet recipes, and a good example is *tortada* (a large pie, usually round in shape with a sponge base) and the *brazo de gitano* ("gypsy's arm" roll). The *tortada* is covered in meringue and decorated with other ingredients, such as egg yolk and sugar, and fruit. The *brazo de gitano* is rolled with a filling of egg yolk and sugar, or custard cream, and then decorated with meringue. Nowadays meringue is often substituted by whipped cream.

1. *Amargos*. Made of ground almond, sugar and egg whites, their origin is uncertain, although they possibly come from mainland Spain. They are typical Christmas pastries.

2. *Carquinyols*. These biscuits made in Mercadal are very popular, but they can be found all over the island. They are made of a dry, firm paste in a square shape, mixing almond, sugar, eggs and flour.

3. *Mantegades*. Best known by their Spanish name, *mantecados*, they consist of almond, egg, flour and lard mixed together. They are not authentically Minorcan, but they can be found in many bakeries and cake shops.

4. *Pastissets* (small cakes). These small cakes are made from sugar, lard, egg yolk and flour in the shape of flower petals. Typically eaten during the Christmas season.

5. *Coca amb roes*. Flour, yeast and sugar in a paste mixed with *roes* (pork scratchings), pieces of pork fat left behind once the lard has been extracted. These are minced and warmed up and then added to the dough.

6. *Coca bamba.* The dough is firm and risen, in the shape of an ensaimada (spiral). It is usually eaten together with hot thick drinking chocolate, and is very popular during holidays and celebrations.

1

2

3   4

5   6

7 8

9 10

59

7. *Ensaimada.* The traditional recipe includes flour,
water, sugar, eggs, yeast
and lard; and can be filled
with sweet shredded
pumpkin, custard cream
or *sobrassada.*

8. *Crespellines.* Small,
dry pastries with an
indented edge, thin but
solid, easy to preserve.

9. Apricot *coca.* Fruit
cocas, such as the apricot
or cherry ones, using the
same base dough as that
of the *coca bamba*. They
can be served in small
pieces in individual por-
tions or may come in a

larger size, either round or
square.

10. Alaior biscuits.
Neither too soft nor too
hard, they are excellent for
dipping in milk. Alaior biscuits are made of flour,
yeast, sugar, oil and water
boiled with aniseed, which
results in a very special
aroma. Before baking in
the oven the middle is
slightly flattened for the
edges to rise more than
the centre.

11. *Crespells*. Easily recognized by their shape: a
star with rounded points
and a central hole. Another
distinguishing trait is the
filling, usually fruit jam of
different varieties but also
cottage cheese, *suquet*
(egg whites with sugar) or
sobrassada.

**12. *Macarrons de
Ciutadella.*** Made with egg
whites and icing sugar,
very sweet. Ground toast-
ed almond can be added.

11 12

1

2

In the pantry

1. Capers. For as long as people can remember, capers have been a wild fruit ready to be picked on limestone cliffs and old walls.

The Minorcan caper is small and hard. When pickled it is very good for accompanying meals and it is used especially in the preparation of a dish made using tongue. The *alcaparrón* – big caper – is in fact the real fruit of the plant, and also very much appreciated and consumed in Minorca. The pickled caper preserve is still made in the traditional way.

2. Honey. This is a very valuable produce in Minorca. It has even been said that Minorcan honey is one of the best in the world; according to the "De re cibaria" book, in the 14th century the king would request honey to be brought from Minorca. Honey combines well with toasted or fried *sobrassada*. There are quite a few beekeepers on the island and they use many different flower varieties for the bees to dispose of a broad spectrum with which to make better honey.

3. *Escopinyes gravades*. These are "embossed clams", on the large side, with deep wide grooves on the shell. They are usually eaten raw with just a few drops of lemon, but they can also be baked in the oven with grated bread and parsley.

3

4   5

6   7

4. *Tomàtics de penjar*. These hanging tomatoes, or *ramellet* tomatoes, take their name from the way in which they are preserved: tied together in a string, they hang from the beams of cool and dry rooms, away from the ground and out of reach of animals and insects.

5. **Camomile.** This is a very much liked wild flower. The camomile growing in La Mola (or Maó) is famous, and part of it is exported. Its use is basically for infusions, as it has antiseptic effects and digestive properties.

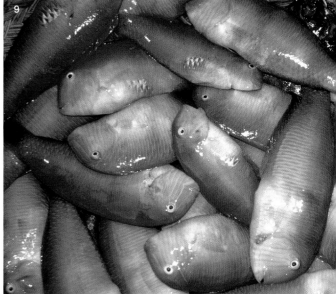

6. **Chocolate.** There are two main chocolate varieties on the island. *Chocolate a la piedra* (very hard, bitter plain chocolate), made of cocoa paste, rice flour and sugar ground and mixed together is used for covering in cakes and sweet pastries, or for making thick drinking chocolate. The other type of chocolate is the **chocolate de neu** (snow chocolate), more typically Minorcan, that comes with a white filling (hence its name) made of boiled, textured sugar and vanillin.

7. *Figat.* Minorcan cuisine includes fruit or vegetable preserves, sweet in taste owing to the great amount of sugar used in the process. Syrups and preserves can be made of melon peel, pumpkin, tomato, peach, lemon, orange… More specifically, *figat* is made of figs cooked for a long time until the texture of soft pulp is obtained. Theoretically sugar should not be added, as the fruit contains more than enough.

8. *Vi de la terra* (local wine). More than a century ago there were good vineyards in Minorca that came to be abandoned for a number of reasons, amongst which we know of the phylloxera pest. Viticulture and wine-making are recently recovered activities, and currently there are cellars making and selling wine. Part of the wine produced comes under the "*Vi de la Terra. Illa de Menorca*" quality certificate. In order to qualify for this honour, the grape varieties used for white wine must be chardonnay, maccabean, malvasia, muscat, parellada and molar. In the case of red wine, it must be cabernet sauvignon, merlot, monastrell (mourvèdre), tempranillo and syrah.

9. *Raors.* This fish is very much appreciated by the locals, eaten after covering in flour and frying. It goes as well by the names of *galán* or *lorito*. The body is extremely compact, with a raised head and powerful teeth. Because of it being so popular, authorities had to limit abusive fishing of the species.

01

serves four

starters

oliaigua amb figues
traditional tomato soup with figs

600g small ripe tomatoes

1 green pepper

1 big onion

4 tbsp olive oil

3 heads of garlic

1¼ litre water

3 bread slices

2 parsley sprigs

salt

8 fresh figs

1- Cut the tomatoes, onions, garlic and pepper into medium pieces and put into a clay pot (a "*tià*" see *vocabulary*).

2- Simmer until glazed according to taste. You can add a little water to prevent sticking or burning.

3- Cover with water and heat but never let it boil. Remove from heat when a white froth forms on the surface.

4- Each person places first some bread in his or her dish and pours the soup on top. Serve with fresh peeled figs.

This dish can be made during the whole year, but this version is the summer one because of the figs. The bread you add to the soup is usually black or a round loaf, slightly dry or toasted. The type of tomatoes can also change according to the season or each person's taste.

caldereta de llagosta
lobster soup

* 2 lobsters weighing 1 kg each * 300 g ripe tomatoes * 3 onions * 1/2 green pepper
* 2 cloves of garlic * 6 tbsp olive oil * 2 tbsp sugar * 2 parsley sprigs * 100g bread
* 1.5 litre mineral water

1- Peel and chop the onions, garlic and tomatoes separately; wash the green pepper and chop as well. Heat the oil in a clay pot (a "tià" (see vocabulary)), and then fry the pepper and onion in it until they start getting transparent then add the tomato and sugar. Leave to simmer slowly for 15 minutes, remove from heat, leave to cool then beat in blender.

2- Cut the lobsters when alive, use a chopping wood and first separate the head from the tail. Set aside the lobster with its juices in a bowl.

3- Remove the black intestine that goes along the tail. The easiest way is to hold with a piece of kitchen paper or cloth and pull slowly to avoid breaking.

4- Remove eggs if there are any, cut the tail in slices, separate legs from trunk. Remove coral coloured intestines with a spoon and chop the head in two parts lengthwise taking care to keep the piece intact and with its juices.

5- Heat the clay pot (a "tià" (see vocabulary)), add the fried vegetables and the pieces of lobster with its previously filtered juice, and cover with water; add the parsley, salt and leave to cook at high heat until it starts to boil, reduce the heat and leave for 30 minutes.

6- Beat the eggs, intestines and garlic in a mortar; add the rest of the juice or some mineral water if the juice is finished. Pour everything in the soup; cook for 5 more minutes and leave to settle before serving.

7- When serving, place bread at the bottom of the dish, cover with the broth, served very hot and add pieces of lobster on top.

In Minorca you can find two types of lobster, the rock one, smaller and bright red, very tasty because of the food rich in essential elements they consume; and the deep water ones, which are bigger, lighter in colour and less tasty due to the meagre food they find in the depths where they live. In both cases the favourites are the females and the best season is summer when the lobsters are full of the eggs that will give more taste to the dish.

esclata-sangs amb salsa
lactarius
mushrooms in sauce

1kg lactarius mushrooms

2 tbsp olive oil

2 tbsp lard

200g *sobrassada*

1 slice of round loaf of bread

1 parsley sprig

1dry bay leaf

1 teaspoon dry thyme

1 teaspoon dry marjoram

1 pinch pepper

1 dl water

1- Clean mushrooms, using a cloth or a brush to remove earth. If the mushrooms are big, cut them in medium pieces.

2- Wash and dry the parsley, strip the leaves and chop. Toast bread until golden. Heat water.

3- Place in mixing bowl, the *sobrassada* in pieces, half of the parsley, the bay leaf in pieces and the dry herbs; add the bread and crush. Wet with warm water and add pepper; stir until you get a thick sauce. Set aside.

4- Mix the lard with oil and when warm fry the mushrooms at high heat for 5 minutes. Add the sauce, reduce heat and leave for 10 more minutes.

"*Esclata sang*" is the Minorcan name of the lactarius mushroom; it is well appreciated served "*as caliu*" which means grilled in red-hot coal and also cooked with meats and game. This mushroom, like many others, must not be cleaned using water: a 2cm wide brush is the best tool to remove earth.

carabassons plens
stuffed courgettes

4 small, white courgettes

2 eggs

2 ripe tomatoes

2 cloves of garlic

4 tbsp breadcrumbs

1 teaspoon salt

6 tbsp olive oil

1- Remove stalk from the courgettes and wash the skin, cut in half lengthwise and boil for ten minutes in salted water. Rinse in cold water and leave to dry flat on kitchen paper or a cloth.

2- Empty them using a spoon, leaving 1/2 cm wall around. Beat the eggs. Chop the courgette pulp, tomato and garlic separately.

3- Heat 4 tbsp oil in a pan and fry the tomato and the garlic lightly (if you like you can also fry chopped spring onions). Leave to simmer for 15 minutes and add the courgette pulp; add salt and cook for 5 more minutes.

4- Remove the pan from heat and mix the fried vegetables with 3 tbsp of breadcrumbs and the eggs. Pre-heat oven to 160º C.

5- Stuff the courgettes with the mixture, place them in an oven tray and sprinkle with the rest of the breadcrumbs.

6- Spray with the rest of the oil and place in the centre of the oven for 30 minutes.

To prepare this dish, you need to use white courgettes from the island; they should be medium or small sized as they have fewer seeds than bigger ones. Choose them firm.

perol de tomàtic

tomatoes in the oven

1 kg tomatoes

1 kg potatoes

4 heads of garlic

2-3 parsley sprigs

8 tbsp olive oil

2 tbsp breadcrumbs

1 tbsp sugar

1- 1- Peel and cut the potatoes in medium slices, wash the tomatoes and cut them in slices. Wash, dry and strip the leaves from the parsley, peel the cloves of garlic and remove core, chop them and mix with breadcrumbs.

2- Pre-heat oven to 180ºC. Place the vegetables in separate layers in a clay pot (a "*tià*" (see *vocabulary*)); start with potatoes, placing the slices one on top of the other.

3- Then place the tomatoes in the same way, to cover the potatoes. Salt and sprinkle with sugar. According to the size of the pot we may have to set up several layers. Finally sprinkle breadcrumbs over the mixture and spray with oil.

4- Put in oven for 40 minutes; then bring the heat down to 140ºC for another 20 minutes.

This is a classical dish of the Minorcan cuisine and it can be eaten either cold or warm. This version can be served with meat or fish, but you can also make a main dish of it putting either meat, squid, prawns or other ingredients between layers.

albergínies as forn
aubergines in the oven

* 4 aubergines * 300 g minced meat (half veal, half pork) * 2 cloves of garlic * 1 dry bay leaf * 50g butter * 100g flour * 1/2 litre full cream milk * 1 pinch nutmeg * 1/2 kg peeled tomatoes * 16 tbsp olive oil * 1 teaspoon salt * 1 tbsp sugar * 50g dry Mahon cheese

1- Cut the aubergines lengthwise in medium slices, place them in a strainer, salt and leave to settle. Grate the cheese.

2- For the béchamel, heat the milk on a low heat, melt the butter in a pan at medium heat, add 40 g of flour and while stirring continuously add the milk. Salt, sprinkle with nutmeg and reduce the heat. Cook for 10 minutes and set aside.

3- Make a tomato sauce cooking the chopped tomatoes in a pan with 4 tbsp of olive oil, salt and sugar for 30 minutes over low heat.

4- Peel and chop the garlic after having removed its core, mix it with the meat and stir fry for 15 minutes with 4 tbsp of olive oil and the chopped bay leaf. Add 3-4 spoonfuls of béchamel and set aside.

5- Place the remaining oil in a pan and when hot fry the aubergines; when done place them on kitchen paper.

6- Spread meat on one end of the aubergine slice and roll it. Repeat with all the aubergines.

7- Put some béchamel and tomato sauce at the bottom of the casserole but do not mix the 2 sauces. Place the aubergine rolls in layers, pouring the sauces in between layers.

8- Start oven grill, sprinkle with cheese and heat under the broiler until brown.

This recipe can be made with different fillings, like fish or meat with fried vegetables (onions, tomatoes and garlic). Some people prefer cutting the aubergines in halves, boiling them quickly, emptying them and filling them with the mixture of meat and chopped aubergine pulp.

carabassa amb guixons
pumpkin
with "guixons" (minorcan beans)

* 1kg pumpkin * 400g "guixons" (beans) * 6 heads of garlic * 2 tbsp flour * 3 parsley sprigs * 6 tbsp olive oil * 1 sweet green pepper* 1 tbsp vinegar

1- The previous day, put the beans to soak and cut the pumpkin in two. Remove seeds and threads and cut in medium slices. Put in strainer, sprinkle with salt and leave it to purge.

2- The next day, place the beans in cold salted water and cook them at low heat for 20 minutes. Then drain them and cook them again in the same way for 20 to 40 minutes.

3- Peel and remove core from garlic, place them in mortar and crush with the pestle with flour adding the oil at the same time, as to make aioli.

4- Mix the pumpkin and garlic paste thoroughly in a mixing bowl. Pre-heat oven to 160ºC.

5- Place the pumpkin slices flat in clay pot (a "*tià*" (see *vocabulary*)) and cook in oven for 1 hour.

6- Once the beans are cooked, drain them, if you want you can also add some chopped sweet green pepper, either raw or slightly sauté and a squirt of vinegar. Serve with the pumpkin.

"*Guixons* "can also be found in Catalonia and Valencia. Contrary to other pulses, "*guixons*" need to be cooked in salted water.

ous amb fesols
eggs with green peas

4 eggs

300g green peas

4 dl stock or water

2 tomatoes

1 green pepper

2 onions

4 cloves of garlic

1 parsley sprig

1 tbsp sugar

salt

1- Boil the eggs in water for 10 minutes. Set aside. Peel and chop the onions, garlic and tomatoes and fry them slightly for 10 minutes in a pan with oil.

2- Wash, dry and chop the parsley. Add the stock to the fried vegetables and cook for 10 minutes, add the peas and heat for 10 more minutes.

3- Remove egg shells, cut eggs in 4, sprinkle the parsley over the peas, add salt and serve with the eggs on top.

As often happens in cooking, there are several versions of each dish; here you can add new potatoes to the fried vegetables and the stock before adding the peas, which have to be fresh and just shelled.

macarrons amb grevi
macaroni with gravy

500g macaroni

1/2 litre meat stock

200g grated Mahon cheese

1 onion

2 tomatoes

1 green pepper

3 cloves of garlic

1 parsley sprig

4 tbsp olive oil

salt

1- Fry the onion, tomato, and the peeled and chopped garlic lightly. Leave to simmer 15 minutes with a pinch of salt and parsley. Strain and set aside the juice. Pre-heat oven to 200ºC.
2- Boil the macaroni in salted water until al dente, strain and mix with the juice kept aside, place in an oven dish and pour the stock over.
3- Sprinkle with cheese and bake in oven until the cheese is golden.

This recipe probably comes from the period when the British ruled the island, as *grevi* is gravy, the English term meaning the juices from roasted meat.

arròs de la terra
country rice

400g coarse ground wheat

100g white "*butifarrón*" (special sausage) (see vocabulary)

100g sobrassada

100g pork ribs

100g streaky bacon or bacon fat

100g black "*butifarrón*" (special sausage) (see vocabulary)

200g sweet potatoes or potatoes

1 head of garlic

2 ripe tomatoes

2 tbsp olive oil

1 teaspoon salt

1- Put the wheat to soak for 8 hours in cold water using a big salad bowl as the wheat will double its size.

2- Strain the wheat, peel and cut the sweet potato and tomatoes. Peel the outer layers of the garlic dry skin, keeping the head in one piece.

3- Cut the meat and sausages (one piece of each, for each person). Pre-heat oven to 160ºC.

4- Place the wheat in a clay pot (a "*tià*" (see *vocabulary*)) and pour the rest of the ingredients on top, placing the head of garlic in the middle. Salt and add the oil. Bake in oven for 45 minutes.

Even if the name of this dish speaks of rice, the principal ingredient is wheat ground coarsely in a stone mortar. According to "De re cibaria" it is a cuisine heritage from the Arabs that has been readapted and is traditionally served in Minorca´s countryside on pig slaughtering day.

02

serves four

main dishes with fish

pagell as forn

red sea bream in the oven

1 kg red sea bream

4 tbsp breadcrumbs

1 tbsp sweet paprika

2 cloves of garlic

2 parsley sprigs

1 teaspoon salt

1/2 litre olive oil

1- Clean the fish inside and outside taking away all the guts and scales. Cut away the fins.

2- Salt inside and outside. Set aside

3- Peel the cloves of garlic and remove core. Wash and dry the parsley, cut leaves finely and crush with the garlic.

4- Mix the sweet paprika with the breadcrumbs in a bowl, add salt and oil; then the crushed garlic and parsley.

5- Pre-heat oven to180ºC. Cover the fish completely with the bread paste, put in an oven tray and cook for 25 minutes.

This way of preparing fish is very common in Minorca. The bread and oil crust not only protects but also gives flavour. You can serve it with tomatoes and potatoes baked in oven (see starters) or you can also slice some potatoes, fry them and place under the fish before baking.

pilotes de cap-roig
scorpion fish balls

* 1 kg scorpion fish, clean * 3/4 kg small fishes for the soup * 50g grated dry Mahon cheese * 1 bay leaf * 3 parsley sprigs * 3 eggs * 3 tbsp breadcrumbs * 1 pinch of tarragon * 1 pinch of marjoram * 1 lemon * 1 dl white wine * 6 tbsp olive oil * 2 tomatoes 2 onions * 1 pinch of cooking salt

1- Cut the fish head and place in a pan with the clean small fishes, the bay leaf, parsley sprig, a peeled onion and a pinch of cooking salt. Cover with water, bring to the boil and simmer for 30 minutes.

2- Add the scorpion fish and cook for 5 more minutes, remove and leave to cool away from the soup. Peel and finely chop the onion and tomato with no seeds. Squeere the lemon and strain.

3- Once washed, chop the parsley leaves. Peel and crumble the fish, mix with the parsley, breadcrumbs and cheese. If necessary add salt to taste.

4- Separate the egg whites from 2 eggs and mix them with a whole egg and 3 tbsp of olive oil, add to the fish and mix until you get a smooth paste.

5- Wet your hands and make little balls slightly oval of the size of a walnut. Strain the broth.

6- Heat the rest of the oil and fry the chopped onion and tomato lightly. Simmer for 15 minutes and add the broth and lemon juice. Turn up the heat and boil for 15 more minutes.

7- Add the balls to the pan and cook for another 5 minutes over medium heat.

8- Thicken the sauce adding the rest of the egg yolk with which you will previously have mixed 2 tbsp of soup, stir well whilst shaking the pan.

This recipe, with its soft flavour and delicate aromas can also be made with fish for soup. In Minorca there is a tradition for fish balls and you can usually find recipes for different sizes of balls made of octopus, squid and many other fish.

bacallà "ab burrida"
cod

1/2 k desalted dried cod

4 cloves of garlic

2 eggs

1/2 litre olive oil

1 pinch of sweet paprika

salt

1- Wash and cut the cod in 4 or 8 pieces (same size), place in a pan, cover with cold water and cook at high temperature.

2- Remove from heat just before it starts boiling (this is when a white froth forms on the surface). Leave to cool in the same water.

3- Separate egg yolks from whites, peel and crush the garlic, remove core if necessary, and prepare an aioli beating yolks and garlic together with some salt and adding at the same time 1/4 litre of oil.

4- Once the fish has cooled down, remove from water (set some of the cooking water aside). Peel and take bones away trying not to make it crumble.

5- Dilute the aioli with some spoonfuls of the cod stock.

6- Put the rest of the oil in a pan and when hot, fry the pieces of fish quickly and serve with the sauce.

The word *burrida* (according to Pedro Ballester) or *borrida* has a lot in common with a Provencal recipe from the south of France called *bourride*. It is a fish soup that you strain just after cooking and then thicken with aioli.

molls amb salsa de fetge
red mullets with liver sauce

* 8 medium red mullets * 1 small egg * 1 teaspoon sweet paprika * 1 onion * 2 heads of garlic * 1 parsley sprig * 1 pinch of dry aromatic herbs * 2dl water * salt * flour * 1/4 litre oil

1- Clean the fish, remove the guts and scales and keep the livers. Wash and leave to strain. Peel and chop the onion, garlic and the parsley previously washed and dried.

2- Heat 4 spoonfuls of oil in a pan, when warm, stir fry the onion, garlic and parsley for 5 minutes, add herbs and sweet paprika.

3- Add water and cook for 5 more minutes. Strain and set aside. Salt the fish and roll in flour, bang gently on the table to remove the excess of flour.

4- Heat the oil in a pan and when warm, fry the fish, 1 minute on each side. When cooked, put in the pan with the sauce.

5- Separate egg yolk and set aside. Fry the livers and crush in a mixing bowl with the egg yolk.

6- Heat the pan, then remove from heat and add the crushed liver. Stir and shake the pan to mix it all.

The best aromatic herbs for this dish are fennel, marjoram and tarragon; you can mix them together or use just two of them. Red mullets should weigh around 100gr. each; they may be not as fine as smaller ones but the liver needs to be big enough to be tasty.

rajada al forn amb patates
ray in the oven with potatoes

1kg clean and chopped ray

1kg potatoes

4 ripe tomatoes

4 heads of garlic

2 parsley sprigs

4 tbsp breadcrumbs

8 tbsp olive oil

1dl water

1 pinch of ground black pepper

salt

1- Peel and cut the potatoes in medium slices. Wash and cut the tomatoes in slices.

2- Wash the parsley and strip the leaves, peel the garlic, crush all together and add the breadcrumbs.

3- Pre-heat oven to 180º C. Cover the bottom of a clay pot (a "*tià*" (see *vocabulary*)) with a layer of potatoes, then put the fish on top, salt, cover with the rest of the potatoes and salt again.

4- Put the tomatoes on top and pour the olive oil and the water over.

5- Sprinkle with the crushed mixture prepared before and pepper. Bake in oven for 40 minutes.

Ray is very much appreciated on the island. We normally eat the fins, but the liver is also delicious. When you buy it, ask the fishmonger to cut and peel it as the ray has a very hard central bone and is covered with several layers of skin similar to the monk fish.

gerrets en escabetx
atherine in vinegar marinade

1kg atherine (Mediterranean type of sardine)

1 onion

1dl olive oil

1dl vinegar

1 head of garlic

1 dry bay leaf

1 tbsp ground black pepper

salt

flour

1- Peel and cut the onion in strips, remove the first layers of dry skin from the head of garlic but leave it whole.

2- Heat the oil in a frying pan and add all the ingredients except the vinegar, and salt. Cook for 5 minutes over low heat.

3- Add the vinegar and cook at high temperature for 10 minutes. Remove from heat.

4- Clean the fish, salt and roll in flour, bang gently on the table to remove the excess of flour. Heat the oil and fry. Place in the marinade and leave for 1 day before eating.

This special sardine (atherine) is very much appreciated in Minorca, but be careful not to get mixed up with the *gerret fabiol* or *anglès*, much more common and less valued, whose back is pink or reddish, instead of being bluish grey, and the belly is whiter.

calamars plens
stuffed squids

1kg medium squids

400g minced meat (half veal, half pork)

50g *sobrassada*

2 cloves of garlic

2 parsley sprigs

6 tbsp breadcrumbs

2 eggs

1dl whole milk

1dl water

4 tbsp olive oil

salt

toothpicks

1- Clean the inside of the squids. Get rid of the innards but keep the tentacle and fins. Chop them. Peel and crush the garlic and the parsley previously washed.

2- Salt the chopped tentacles and mix with the garlic, parsley, breadcrumbs and egg.

3- Crumble the sobrassada and add it to the mixture. Mix thoroughly until the mixture is smooth. Stuff the squids with the mixture. Close them with toothpicks.

Golden the squids on each side in a pan with warm oil, add milk and water and the rest of the stuffing mixture, and simmer over very low heat for 20 to 30 minutes.

It would be better to use a diffuser to cook this dish as milk usually makes ingredients stick in the pan when the heat is too high. If you do not have any, use more water and less milk.

According to Pedro Ballester it is easy to mix up squid and *aluja* whose meat is tougher and little appreciated.

sípia amb fesols
cuttlefish with green peas

1 kg cuttlefish

400g peas

1 onion

2 tomatoes

4 cloves of garlic

2 parsley sprigs

6 tbsp olive oil

2 tbsp salt

1 dl water

1- Clean the cuttlefish, set the liver and the tentacles aside, and throw out the innards. Cut the body and the tentacles in pieces.

2- Cook the cuttlefish in a clay pot (a "*tià*" (see *vocabulary*)) for 30 minutes with no liquid so it expels all its water. Remove from heat and set aside.

3- Peel and chop the onion, garlic and parsley leaves once they have been cleaned and dried with a cloth or kitchen roll.

4- In the same clay pot fry the onion, garlic and parsley. Pour some water in and add the peas, the cuttlefish and its crushed liver. Simmer for 1 hour. Salt and bring to the boil once just before serving.

This dish is very well known; you can easily find it as a *tapa* in the island's bars. There is a more complete version with meatballs. The cuttlefish liver is the brown bag you find inside the cuttlefish and even though it is not always used, it is the liver which really gives the flavour to this dish.

pop amb ceba
octopus with onion

1kg octopus

500g onion

6 tbsp olive oil

1dl water

1 tbsp salt

1- The previous day, clean the octopus, remove ink and freeze the octopus. The next day, defreeze and cut it, separate head and tentacles.

2- Heat a clay pot and cook the octopus for 30 minutes with no liquid so it can expel its own water. Leave it to cool down.

3- Peel the onion and cut it in julienne. Cut the octopus tentacles in 2cm slices and the rest in bigger pieces.

4- Fry the octopus in a clay pot (a "*tià*" (see *vocabulary*)) in oil for 10 minutes on a high light, add the onion, mix and cook for 10 more minutes.

Add water and after bringing it to the boil, turn the heat down and simmer gently for 1 hour. Salt and bring to the boil before serving.

We recommend freezing the octopus and the cuttlefish so they are more tender and do not need to be beaten. Some recommend cooking it first in water with some bay leaves and leaving it to cool down in the same water, rather than of cooking it with no liquid.

caragols amb cranca
snails with spider crabs

* 1kg cleaned snails * 1/2 kg spider crabs and crabs legs and claws * bouquet garni (carrot, celery, leek, turnip) * 1/2 green pepper * 1 onion * 3 ripe tomatoes * 2 head of garlic * 2dl white wine * 1 chilli pepper * 4tbsp olive oil * salt

1- The previous day, wash the snails and put them in a pan to cook over low heat for 30 minutes, with the vegetables, 1tbsp salt and covered with cold water. Leave to cool in their water.

2- Cut the crabs in two halves. Peel and chop the onion and garlic finely. Chop the green pepper and tomatoes.

3- Heat the oil in a clay pot (a "*tià*" (see *vocabulary*)) and fry the chopped vegetables. Cook over low heat for 15 minutes and add the chilli, crabs, legs and claws. Salt, pour in the wine and cook at a high temperature for 10 more minutes.

4- Strain the snails; add them to the sauce with a ladle of stock and leave to cook at high temperature for 10 to 15 minutes. Remove from heat, leave to cool down at room temperature. Consume the next day.

This recipe was made with "*crancs peluts*", which nowadays is a protected species of crab. Some people prepare it with "*cranca*", spider crab, crushing its guts as it gives a lot of taste to the dish. Others like to thicken it with a slice of toasted round loaf.

serves four

main dishes with meat

cocs farcits
stuffed rolls

8 rolls from the previous day

1/2 kg of different kind of sausages from the island

2dl full cream milk

50gr lard

twine

1- Cut the sausages in medium slices. Open the rolls lengthwise and soak them in milk for a few minutes. Take the lard out of the refrigerator to soften it.

2- Leave the rolls to strain before filling one half with slices of sausage. Close with the other half and tie them with the twine.

Pre-heat oven to 200ºC. Spread a small amount of lard all over the buns, place them in an oven tray and bake for 15 minutes.

Traditionally, these rolls were prepared on Christmas Eve before Midnight Mass. As always there are several versions of the dish, one of which is to empty the buns or rolls of their crumbs and stuff them with a mixture of pork meat, *sobrassada* and some of the crumb previously soaked.

These rolls or "*cocs*" are normally quite long and according to their size, one or two are usually served per person.

pilotes a la menorquina

minorcan style meat balls

* 1kg minced meat (half veal, half pork) * 50g *sobrassada* * 2 eggs * 3 cloves of garlic * 1 onion * 4 tbsp breadcrumbs * 3 parsley sprigs * 1 pinch of thyme * 1/2 kg ripe tomatoes * 2 tbsp pine nuts * 1 green pepper * 1 bay leaf * 3 tbsp olive oil * 3 teaspoons sugar * 1 teaspoon salt

1- Peel and chop the onion and 2 cloves of garlic. Wash and cut the pepper in pieces. Wash, peel and remove seeds from the tomatoes and crush them. Wash the parsley and chop the leaves. Beat the eggs.

2- Pre-heat oil in clay pot (a "*tià*" (see *vocabulary*)) and fry onion and pepper for 5 minutes. Add garlic, cook for 5 minutes and then add the tomato, salt, sugar and bay leaf. Reduce heat; add the pine nuts and leave to simmer over low heat for 30 more minutes.

3- Crumble the *sobrassada* and mix it with the meat, salt. Peel and chop the rest of the garlic without its core and add it to the meat with the parsley, thyme, breadcrumbs and eggs. Beat well until the mixture is smooth.

Mix the sauce. With wet hands roll the meat balls (about 1,5cm in diameter). Fry until golden in hot oil for about 2 minutes and add them to the sauce. Simmer all together for 20 more minutes.

This recipe is also very popular and we can find it served as *tapas* in bars. As always recipes vary from Mahon to Ciudadela, but in this case they all agree to use pine nuts in the sauce.

feixets de vedella
little veal rolls

4 thin veal fillets

25g bacon fat

25g *sobrassada*

2 small eggs

2 ripe tomatoes

vegetable mix for soup (carrot, celery, leek, turnip)

4 tbsp olive oil

1 teaspoon sugar

2 teaspoon salt

twine

1- Boil the eggs for ten minutes. Chop the bacon and the *sobrassada* finely. Chop the tomatoes.

2- Cool the eggs and peel them, cut them in 4. Cut each veal fillet in two.

3- Spread the stuffing and the eggs on the 8 pieces of meat, roll and tie them.

4- Wash and peel the vegetables and put them in a clay pot (a "*tià*" (see *vocabulary*)) with the veal rolls, tomato and oil. Add water and bring to the boil then leave it to simmer for 45 minutes.

5- Remove meat and strain sauce in the sieve, place the rolls back in the clay pot with the sauce, take off twine and bring to the boil before serving.

The "*feixets*" or rolls which according to Ballester were known as "*perdius de capella*" ("chapel partridges") are very much appreciated in the northern part of the island. It is very important that the meat is very thinly cut and then divided in two to obtain small rolls.

cuixa de be as forn
leg of lamb in the oven

1,5kg whole leg of lamb

300g cured *sobrassada*

100g fresh streaky bacon

1tbsp lard

1 tbsp salt

1 tbsp ground black pepper

1- The previous day, place the streaky bacon and *sobrassada* in the refrigerator to be able to cut them better the next day.

2- Cut the sobrassada in slices, set 100g aside and then cut the rest in strips, cut the streaky bacon in strips too.

3- Stuff the meat puncturing it with a sharp knife. Place a piece of *sobrassada* and one of bacon alternatively in each cut. Salt and pepper each side and keep in refrigerator.

4- Pre-heat oven to 200ºC. Place the rest of the *sobrassada* at the bottom of the clay pot (a "*tià*" (see *vocabulary*)) and the leg of lamb on top.

5- Put little pieces of lard over the leg, turn the oven down to 180ºC and roast for 40 to 50 minutes in the centre of the oven. Remove from oven and leave it to settle before serving.

You can serve this dish with fried potatoes and a fresh tomato salad. You can either fry the potatoes in deep oil or in a mixture of oil and lard; fry them with cloves of garlic and bay leaves.

llenquetes de be amb salsa
lamb pieces with sauce

* 1kg leg of lamb in fillets * 1 tbsp lard * 100g streaky bacon * 2 carrots * 1 parsnip
* 12 pearl onions * 1 parsley sprig * 1 bay leaf * 1 pinch of marjoram * 1dl dry white wine
* 1dl broth * 1 squirt vinegar * salt

1- Peel the onions. Peel and cut the carrots in thick slices and cut the parsnip lengthwise in 4. Wash and chop the parsley leaves.

2- Melt the lard with the bacon in a clay pot (a "*tià*" (see *vocabulary*)) at medium-high temperature. When the bacon is golden remove it from the pot and set aside.

3- Fry the lamb fillet until golden in the fat that is in the pot. When ready, put on a plate and salt.

4- Put the streaky bacon and meat back in the clay pot and add the vegetables, herbs, wine, broth and vinegar.

5- Simmer for 30 to 40 minutes, shaking the casserole from time to time until the sauce has reduced and slightly thickened.

The pearl onions are the ones called French onions in Spain. To prevent their layers from falling apart, you must peel them carefully and leave the peduncle in which its roots are fixed.

llom de porc amb cames-seques
pork loin with chanterelles mushrooms

* 1kg loin of pork * 100g chanterelles mushrooms * 1 big onion * 3 cloves of garlic * 2 pinches of rosemary * 1 bay leaf * 1dl white wine * 1 squirt water * 4 tbsp olive oil * salt * ground black pepper

1- Peel and chop the onion and garlic. Salt and pepper the meat. Clean the mushrooms; if you use dried mushrooms soak them in water. Pre-heat oven to 180°C.

2- Heat the oil in a frying pan and brown the meat until done. Set aside. Use the same oil to fry the onions, garlic and herbs for 5 minutes.

3- Place the meat back in the pot, pour wine and water; add the mushrooms (strained if you have used them dried); bring to the boil and remove from heat.

4- Cover the pot with paper and finish cooking in oven for 50 to 60 minutes. Remove the meat and leave to settle.

5- Strain and reduce the sauce on a high light for 10 minutes and set mushrooms and onions aside. Cut the meat and put it in the pot with the sauce and mushrooms and serve.

The chanterelles are mushrooms you can find fresh in season, but you can use dry ones instead or even dehydrated St George's mushrooms.

peus de porc gratinats
pigs´ trotters in gratin

1/2 kg cooked pigs´ trotters

500g grated Mahon cheese

250g fresh bacon

3 eggs

3 tbsp full cream milk

3 tbsp flour

5 tbsp breadcrumbs

2 tbsp lard

1- Chop the bacon finely. Bone and chop the trotters, mix them with the bacon in a clay pot (a "*tià*" (see *vocabulary*)). Pre-heat oven to 180ºC.

2- Add the cheese to the mixture. Beat eggs and add them, sprinkle with flour and then pour in milk. Stir until you get a smooth dough.

3- Spread some lard in the pot and sprinkle with 2 tbsp breadcrumbs. Add salt to taste and fill the pot with the dough.

Sprinkle the rest of breadcrumbs on top and put the rest of the lard in small lumps on top of it as well. Bake in oven for 30 minutes.

This dish is a very fine one, and not at all greasy as pig trotters are made of gelatine not fat. We advise using low salt cheese.

pollastre amb salsa d'ametlles
chicken in almond sauce

1kg chicken cut in pieces

100 g chopped almonds

2 cloves of garlic

25 g round loaf

6 tbsp oil

1 pinch of dry oregano

1 pinch of ground black pepper

4 dl water

flour

salt

1- Toast bread. Peel garlic cloves, remove core and crush with bread in mortar, mix with almond and dilute with water. Set aside.

2- Heat the oil in a clay pot (a "*tià*" (see *vocabulary*)), salt and pepper chicken, roll in flour and fry until golden.

3- Add the almond paste and simmer for 30 minutes. Shake the casserole from time to time so the sauce thickens and does not stick at the bottom.

We recommend cutting the chicken in 8 pieces. If you prefer you can buy whole almonds and crush them yourself in the mortar or use a blender with the toasted bread and garlic.

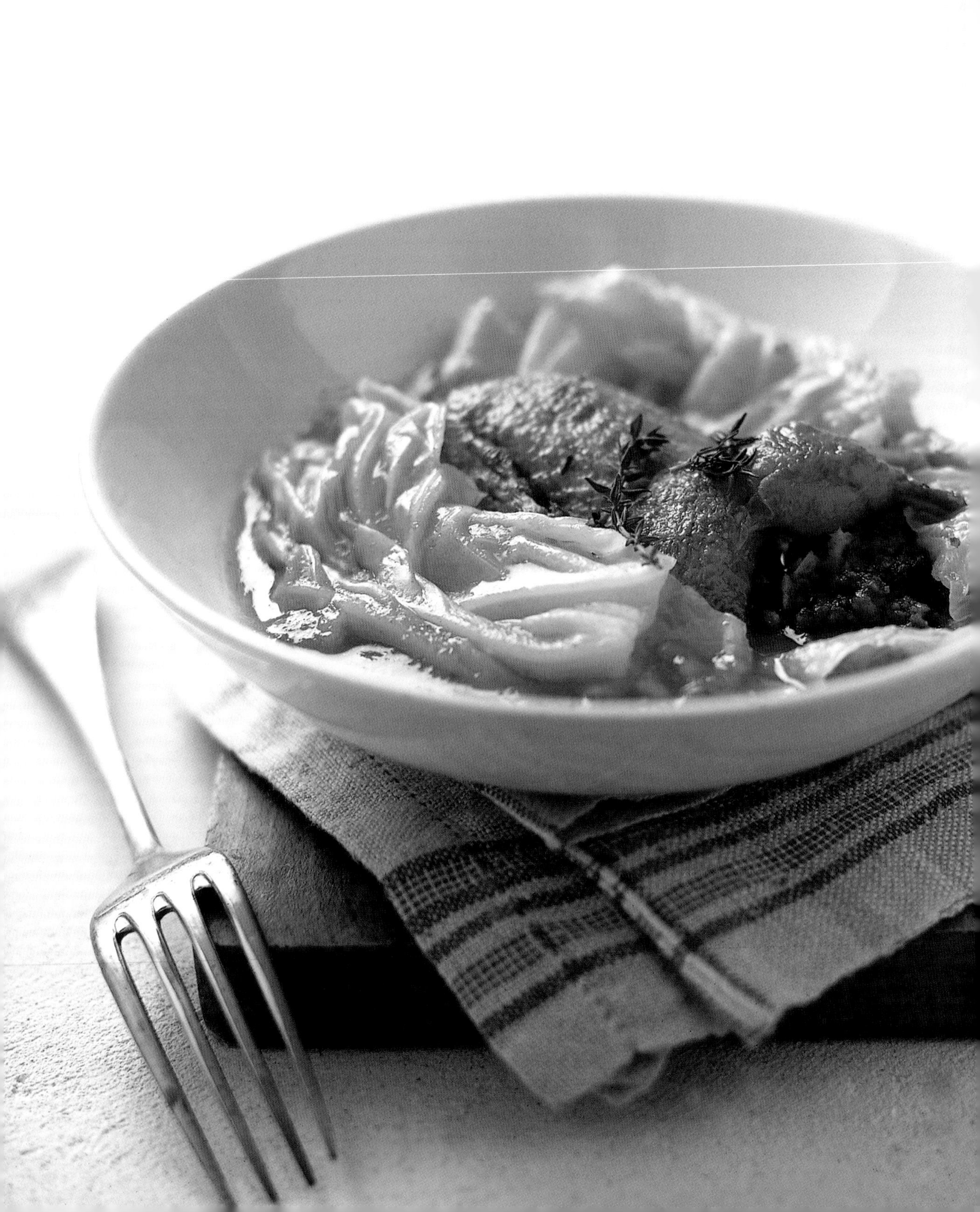

perdius amb col
partridges with green cabbage

* 4 partridges * 8 outer leaves of green cabbage * 50g bacon fat * 50 g *butifarró negre* (black sausage) * 50g *sobrassada* * 50g streaky bacon * 1 dl white wine * bouquet garni (carrot, celery, leek, turnip) * 1 onion * 1 pinch ground black pepper * 2 dl water or broth salt * twine

1- Peel and chop the onion and the soup vegetables. Blanch the cabbage leaves in salted water for 1 minute and put in cold water to cool down. Make 4 parts of the sausages and streaky bacon.

2- Melt the bacon fat in a pot. Salt and pepper the partridges and stuff them with a piece of each sausage and one of streaky bacon then fry them on a high light for 2 minutes on each side.

3- Strain the cabbage leaves and roll each partridge in one or two of them. Close each bundle with twine.

4- Place the pot on the heat; fry the onion for 5 minutes and add the bundle of vegetables. Place the partridges in the pot and add the water and wine, but do not cover all the ingredients. Simmer for 40 minutes.

5- Remove partridges, strain and reduce the sauce for 10 minutes on a high light and serve.

If you like you can also peel and cut all the vegetables which will make a more complete dish. You can also finish cooking the dish in the oven, as many do.

conill amb salsa
rabbit in sauce

1 kg rabbit cut in pieces

150g bacon

1 big onion

1/2 head of garlic

1 bay leaf

1 teaspoon ground black pepper

2 dl sherry

3 tbsp olive oil

1 dl water

1 teaspoon salt

1 tbsp flour

1- Peel and chop the onion and separate the cloves of garlic without peeling them. Cut the bacon in pieces.

2- Heat the oil and fry the pieces of rabbit until golden, then add the bacon.

3- Add the onion and cook for 5 minutes; then add the garlic and bay leaf, salt and pepper.

4- Add the flour to the sherry and mix well then pour in together with the water. Reduce heat and simmer for 30 minutes stirring from time to time to avoid sticking

"De re cibaria" says that the flour should be lightly toasted. To achieve this, toast it in a pan with no liquid, at medium heat and stirring all the time until it gets a light brown colour.

04

serves four

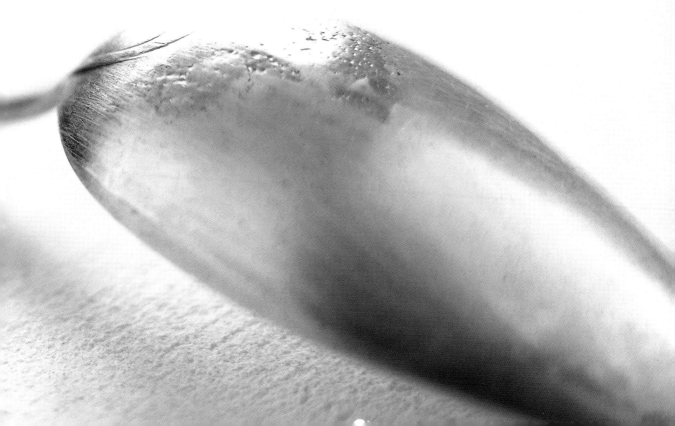

sweets
and desserts

moniatos as forn
sweet potatoes in the oven

500g sweet potatoes

3dl full cream milk

1 teaspoon ground cinnamon

2 tbsp sugar

1- Pre- heat oven to 180ºC. Peel the sweet potatoes and cut in medium or thin slices.

2- Put the slices in a pot (a "*tià*" [see *vocabulary*]), arrange in layers and sprinkle each layer with sugar and cinnamon.

3- Pour in the milk, place in oven and cook for 45 minutes.

The sweet potato ("*monyaco*" in Minorca) is widely used on the island, and it is prepared in salted and sweet dishes as fried dough or puddings. Islanders also prepare this recipe "*as caliu*" (barbecued)

figues as forn
figs in the oven

500g fresh figs

4 tbsp sugar

1 dl water

1- Pre-heat oven to 180ºC. Wash the figs and remove tip.

2- Pour water in a clay pot (a "*tià*" (see *vocabulary*)), place figs in it and sprinkle with sugar.

3- Bake in oven for 30 minutes. Leave to cool down and serve lukewarm, almost cold.

Minorca is known for her numerous fig trees and the abundance of local varieties ("*figaflor*", "*coll de dama*", "*bordissot*", "*paratjal*"…). The first one to ripen, at the end of June is "*figaflor*" the most valued. Others ripen in August ("*agostenques*") and some others in October but it is the summer ones that are most appreciated and that are used in desserts and "*Oliaigua*".

greixera de carabassa
pumpkin pastry

1 kg pumpkin

200g sugar

100g butter

4 eggs

1 tbsp ground cinnamon

1 lemon

1- Cut the pumpkin in pieces, peel and remove seeds. Boil for 30 minutes. Strain in a colander and cover with a piece of cloth until cold.

2- Wash the lemon and grate half its rind (only the yellow part). Melt the butter and beat eggs. Pre-heat oven to 150ºC.

3- Press the pumpkin in the cloth until all the water has been drained, place in a bowl and mix with the sugar, grated lemon and butter.

4- Add the cinnamon and eggs, mix and fill a low pan with this dough. Bake for one hour in the oven (adjust rack to lower position).

It is very important to strain the cooked pumpkin completely before mixing it with the rest of the ingredients. The oven tray or mould must be shallow.

menjar blanc
white custard

1 litre full cream milk

150g sugar

1 lemon

200g rice flour

1 cinnamon stick

1 vanilla bean

1 dl water

1- Wash the lemon and remove half of its rind (try not to get to the white part). Open the vanilla bean lengthwise.

2- Heat the water in a pan with the cinnamon, lemon skin and vanilla.

3- Mix the flour with the milk, add the sugar and heat. Mix it with the cinnamon syrup as soon as it comes to the boil.

4- Reduce heat and simmer stirring all the time until it thickens. If you want thicker custard, you can cook it for a longer time.

5- Place the custard in individual containers and leave to cool down.

This is a dessert inherited from Arab cuisine. You can also make it with cornflour or wheat flour, but it is not as fine with the latter. Some people use orange rind instead of lemon skin.

mel i mantega
honey and butter

400g buns
200g honey from Minorca
100g butter

1- Cut the buns in small pieces or if you use bread from the previous day cut it in thin slices

2- Place the honey and butter in a clay pot (a "*tià*" (see *vocabulary*)) and heat stirring constantly so it does not boil.

3- When all the ingredients are melted, add the bread and bring to the boil. Remove from heat and serve.

You can also serve the dish with the mixture of butter and honey in a gravy boat and the bread apart.

púding
pudding

500g white bread from the previous day

200g sugar

2dl full cream milk

3 eggs

150g sultanas

1 pinch of ground cinnamon

1 lump of butter

1- Soak the sultanas in lukewarm water. Remove crust from bread and cut in pieces. Place it in a bowl, cover with milk and leave to soak until soft.

2- Strain the sultanas, beat the eggs and add them with the sugar and cinnamon to the bread.

3- Pre-heat oven to 180ºC. Grease a pudding or cake mould with butter and fill it with the bread and sultana dough.

4- Bake for 25 to 30 minutes. See if cooked by punching a thin knife in the centre, if it comes out clean the pudding is ready but if not cook for a little longer. Serve lukewarm or cold.

We suppose that this sweet dish, which is also served at teatime, was inherited from the British when they came to the island. There are many other pudding recipes, like potato pudding- with or without almonds- "*ensaimada*" pudding, "*brossat*" (cottage cheese) pudding or egg pudding also called "*flam*" (flan).

coca de congret
sponge cake

6 eggs

250 g sugar

250 g cornflour

1 lemon

1 pinch of salt

1 tbsp lard or butter

Caster sugar

1- Clean the lemon rind. Separate egg yolks and whites, put the egg whites to chill in refrigerator and beat the yolks with sugar until white.

2- Sift the flour and add it to the eggs, while beating. Whisk the egg whites with salt until they form peaks.

3- Pre-heat oven to 160ºC. Grate the rind of a half lemon on top of the eggs, mix and add the egg whites at the same time.

4- Grease a mould with the lard and fill with the dough, leaving enough space for it to rise and cook for 35 to 40 minutes until it gets a golden colour. Sprinkle with caster sugar before serving.

This recipe can also be made in individual egg shaped containers. You can serve it with "*figat*" which is a sweet made of figs cooked with melon rind and aniseed or with the aromatic plant "*batafaluga*" (anise).

orellanes
pancake

1 dl muscatel wine

1 dl olive oil

250g flour

100g honey

oil for frying

flour

1- Mix the oil and wine. Sift the flour and mix with blender until you get a smooth dough.

2- Leave to settle at room temperature for 30 minutes. Melt the honey in bain marie and set aside until it is time to serve.

3- Sprinkle flour on the table and on the rolling pin. Heat a generous quantity of oil in a deep fry pan.

4- Take a lump of dough and spread it, make the pancakes as thin as possible with the rolling pin and pinch the entire surface with a fork.

When the oil starts to smoke, fry the discs of dough until some small bubbles form. Strain on kitchen paper before serving with melted honey.

These pancakes (called "*Oranas*" in Minorca) are very typical in Catalan pastry, even on the French side where they are called "*bugnes*" or "*bunyetes*" depending on the shape or the place they come from.

bunyols de tots sants
easter doughnuts

100g Mahon tender cheese

1 egg

flour

sugar

oil for frying

1- Grate the cheese. Separate egg whites from yolks, keep whites for another recipe and mix yolks with the cheese.

2- Sift the flour on the cheese and mix thoroughly at the same time. Add flour until the dough is thick.

3- Heat a good quantity of oil in a fryer; wet your hands and take pieces of dough with your wet hands. Make balls.

4- Fry the doughnuts all over turning them with a skimming ladle and strain them on kitchen paper. Sprinkle some sugar on top and serve warm.

Pancakes are very much appreciated in the island gastronomy. You can find them in different shapes, but they are generally ring shaped. Ingredients can also vary according to the season. Apart from the Easter doughnuts, there are potato doughnuts, sweet potato doughnuts and dry fig doughnuts.

cuscussó
minorcan bread plum cake

1/2 kg dry round loaf (without salt)

1/2 kg ground almonds

1/2 kg sugar

300g lard

150g crystallised fruits

50g sultanas

50g pine nuts

1 lemon

1 teaspoon ground cinnamon

1- Cut the bread in the thinnest possible slices. Wash and cut the lemon rind, grate it and set aside. Cut the crystallised fruit and golden the pine nuts.

2- Dilute the sugar in 1 dl of boiling water. Add the lard and the sultanas and simmer until you obtain caramel.

3- Sprinkle the cinnamon and the grated lemon rind, mix and add the bread and almonds. Work the mixture for 5 minutes. Remove from heat.

4- Leave the dough to settle for a few minutes until temperatures lowers. Shape into buns before the dough gets cold. Decorate with the crystallised fruit and the pine nuts.

This recipe has an Arab origin and it is also used, without the almond and the fruit, as a stuffing for chicken or turkey.

vocabulary

Caldera (or **Caldereta**). This is one of the most common ways to prepare fish and seafood. The base is of fried vegetables in abundant broth. You can also serve it the way fishermen did, placing all the raw ingredients in cold water and then boiling them all together. Serve with dry or toasted bread. The lobster "*caldereta*" is the most famous of all.

Congret. This is a type of sponge cake and is used as a base for many cakes and tarts that are covered or filled with different ingredients such as chocolate, meringue, cream, jam, egg yolk…

Esclata-sang (lactarius), **girgola** (pleurotus), **cames-seques** (chanterelles). Three native types of mushrooms very commonly used in Minorcan recipes.

Fesol (pea).Minorcan name for peas. In other Catalan speaking regions, **fesols** are a type of bean.

Formatjada. Minorcan pastry, stuffed with *sobrassada*, meat and bacon. Usually eaten during Easter season, it is the most genuine stuffed pastry in the island.

Guixons (Minorcan beans). This small legume, with a black mark on it, is very scarcely used and thus has a very special personality.

Oliaigua (tomato soup with figs). This soup was created in times of scarce food supply, using water, oil and bread. You can add tomato, garlic, green pepper and onion. You serve it with fresh figs.

Panadera. The potato is the principal ingredient of this dish, which like the "*caldereta*" uses fried vegetables and goes with meat, fish or other produce.

Ple o farcit (stuffing or filling). Used for oven preparations. You usually stuff aubergine, courgettes, green pepper, red pepper and squid.

Sèu (lard). This product has been widely used in traditional cuisine, but is currently being replaced by olive oil or butter so as to get lighter and more digestive dishes.

Suquet. Stuffing used for several sweet pastries, like the "*crespell*", and made of egg white and sugar. Do not get mixed up with the fish "*suquet*" which is widely consumed on the Valencia coast.

Tià, perol (clay pot). The most used recipient in Minorcan cuisine. The "*tià*" is a round, shallow clay pot; the "*perol*" is a normally rectangular oven dish which can be made of glass, clay or metal.

Tomàtic de penjar. A type of small tomato, which you hang in strings from the beams of dry and fresh places to enable their conservation.

bibliography

Ballester, Pedro: *De re cibaria*. ISBN: 84-920610-1-4. (1923 First edition). Sixth edition (1995).

Borràs, Josep; Borràs, Damià: *La Cuina dels Menorquins*. Columna Edicions S.A. Second edition (March 2000).

Bonet, Antoni: *Menorca pagesa*. Published by Antoni Bonet. Second edition (1997).

Cavaller Triay, Ramon: *La cuina menorquina (I)*. Col. Quaderns de Folklore, no.14. Published by Col·lectiu Folklòric de Ciutadella (April 1984).

Ripoll, Luis: *Libro de cocina menorquina*. Published by Luis Ripoll Arbós. Second edition (1991).

Bestard, Inmaculada; Cañellas, Jaume; Femenia, Antoni; Rosselló Carme: *Conèixer i gaudir els aliments de les Illes Balears*. Published by the Conselleria d'Agricultura i Pesca del Govern Balear and the Universitat de les Illes Balears. IQUA, Institut de Qualitat Agroalimentària de les Illes Balears.

Fàbrega, Jaume; Puigvert, Carme: *La cuina de Menorca*. Published by La Magrana (1995).

web: www.illesbalearsqualitat.com
www.uib.es/secc6/slg/gt/noms_peixos.html.
dgpesca.caib.es/user/pesca_recreativa/pesca_recreativa.pdf
www.illesbalears.es
www.agroprofesional.com/especiales/baleares04
www.cheesefromspain.com/CFS/1503Mahon_E.htm
www.quesos.com

recipe index
serves four